SUPER SIMPLE QUILTS #6

OPTIKA

KATHLEEN EATON

Chilton Book Company
Radnor, Pennsylvania

To Joe, Joan, Rose, and Chuck
Thank you for your loving support and encouragement.

ACKNOWLEDGMENTS

I'm grateful for the photographic talents of Michael Boburka, who assisted with black-and-white photography, and the artistic talents of Katharine Schwengel, who assisted with line drawings. Special thanks to them and to the many other people who made this book possible, especially Mom and Dad, Barb and Jim, Robbie Fanning, Tim Scott, Nancy Zieman, Jessica, Charlie, David, Tom, Sue, and
the people of the Camera Fair in Marinette, Wisconsin.

INTRODUCTION

The Optika pattern is better known as Tumbling Blocks, and gets its name from the illusion of building blocks that it creates. Despite its intricate appearance, the pattern and instructions for making this quilt will enable you to finish it in less than two days. By experimenting with fabric placement, you can achieve a variety of designs with a single pattern piece.

Whether you are an expert quilter or just beginning to discover the joy and satisfaction of quiltmaking, the Optika was made for you. Now you can custom-make a handcrafted quilt, in sizes from twin to king, that will last for years, at a fraction of the cost of a store-bought comforter, in a fraction of the time you thought it would take. And you can take pride in knowing you did it yourself.

Included with your quilt project are patterns for accessory items: a crib quilt, wall hanging, throw pillow, pillow sham, chair pad, and placemat. Use your imagination and decorate every room in your home!

The secret of successful quilting is . . . Keep It Super Simple!

Published in Radnor, Pennsylvania 19089, by Chilton Book Company

Designed by Anthony Jacobson
Cover photo by Tim Scott
Manufactured in the United States of America

Library of Congress Catalog Card Number 92-53149
ISBN 0-8019-8340-1

1 2 3 4 5 6 7 8 9 0   9 8 7 6 5 4 3 2 1 0

Make a Quilt

In this section you will find all the information you need to make a twin, full, queen, or king-size quilt. Instructions for making a crib-size quilt or wall hanging begin on page 6-9.

Getting Started

Optika, also known as Tumbling Blocks, creates an optical illusion with its shading of the three main pieces. Although Optika is one of the more difficult and intriguing of the Amish patterns, I have enlarged the pattern to simplify it and give it a more contemporary look. For best results, use starkly contrasting light- and dark-colored solid fabrics, with a medium shade or a blend of the dark and light colors, as the third fabric. (For example, try black, white, and gray.) Also dynamic, and great for children's rooms, are royal blue, flame red, and sunshine yellow. The crib quilt is a welcome gift in powder blue, petal pink, and pale yellow. Avoid fabrics with a nap or definite one-way design.

Because equal amounts of fabric are used for each color, I have not designated which fabric should be placed in what position. Rather, it is best to experiment before the initial "Tumbling Blocks" have been pieced, to decide on the layout you prefer. But to achieve the best optical effect, I recommend positioning the blocks in the same direction throughout the quilt.

Materials Needed

Fabric

Yardage amounts listed are what is needed for a quilt only. Refer to the yardage requirements for pillows, pillow shams, etc., as desired, and add accordingly.

Twin (90″ × 68″): 2¾ yards each of three fabrics

Full/queen (90″ × 86″): 3½ yards each of three fabrics

King (90″ × 102″): 4¼ yards each of three fabrics

Batting and Backing

Polyester fiberfill or wool or cotton batting large enough to complete your quilt.

A large, flat sheet or extra-wide fabric, large enough to use as a backing on your quilt. Three yards of 108″ sheeting (available at well-supplied fabric stores) will fit all sizes. Or you can use 44/45″-wide fabric as follows: For twin size, you need 5½ yards of 44/45″ wide fabric, cut into two pieces, each 2¾ yards long. Seam them together along the selvages (Fig. 6-1). For full/queen and king sizes, you need 8¼ yards of 44/45″ wide fabric, cut in three pieces, each 2¾ yards, seamed together along the selvages (Fig. 6-2).

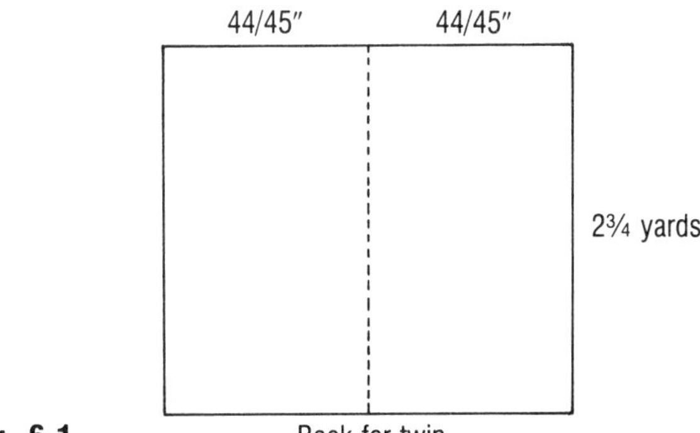

Fig. 6-1

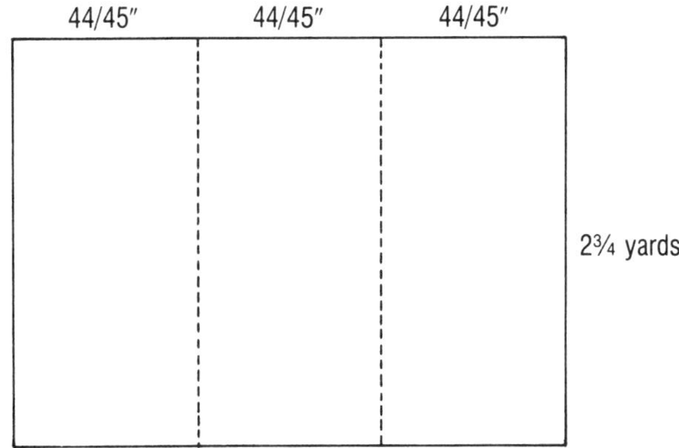

Fig. 6-2

When laying out the backing, batting, and quilt top, center the quilt top so the seams in the back are equal distances from the sides.

Don't Forget

Thread (for piecing your quilt face, as well as for hand or machine quilting, if desired)

String, yarn, or 1/16″ ribbon for tying your quilt, if you prefer

Graph paper or plain paper (which you have scored with 1″ squares) for pattern making

Making the Pattern

The Optika pattern requires only one pattern piece. For the bed-size quilts, you will need to make your own pattern piece using graph paper, gridded freezer paper, or tracing paper taped to a 1″ gridded cutting board. Graph paper is available in a variety of "squares-to-the-inch" sizes. It doesn't matter what size you choose, as long as the 1″ lines are clearly visible. If you are using smaller pieces of graph paper, carefully tape them together using clear tape, making sure the lines match up vertically and horizontally.

Here's how to draw your pattern piece: Start by marking a dot (Dot 1) on the corner of one square on the grid. (See the pattern guide on page 6-15). Now count 16½″ and mark Dot 2, as shown. Draw your solid line from Dot 1 to Dot 3 (11″), then draw your dashed line from Dot 3 to Dot 2 (5½″). Now draw a dashed line, 9½″, from Dot 2 to Dot 4. Draw a solid line across from Dot 4 to Dot 5 (11″). To complete your parallelogram, draw lines between Dots 1 and 5 and between Dots 3 and 4.

Note: Do not add seam allowances. Unlike in some quilt pattern books, the Optika patterns already include a ⅜″ seam allowance.

After you have drawn your pattern piece on the grid, double-check all measurements, and carefully cut it out (Fig. 6-3).

Fig. 6-3

Cutting the Fabric

This pattern is ideal for rotary cutting tools. Lay the fabric flat on a cutting surface, and fold it in half lengthwise, then in half again, also lengthwise. Lay the pattern piece as shown in Fig. 6-4, and carefully cut until you reach the end of the length of fabric. If done carefully, the cut edge of the first piece you cut can be used as a cut edge for the next piece, and so on. The number of pieces needed is given on the pattern guide on page 6-15.

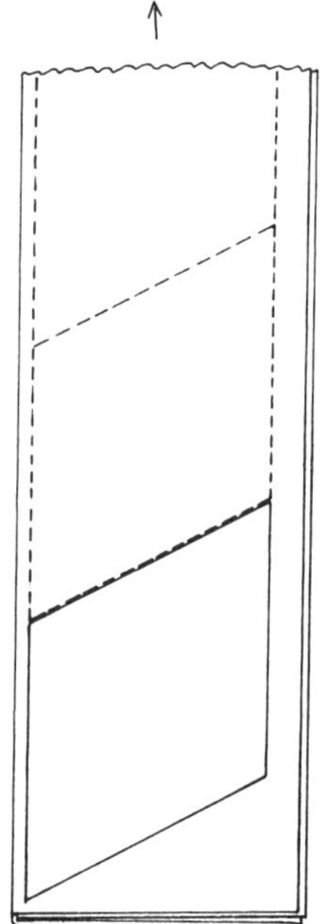

Fig. 6-4

Sewing the "Tumbling Blocks"

Hint #1: When one or both pattern pieces is being sewn on a bias (angle-cut) edge, it helps to pin the edges together to prevent pulling or stretching the fabric. Otherwise, it is not necessary to pin pieces together before sewing them. In fact, it's quicker and easier not to. Just be sure you're letting the machine do the work, and that you're not pulling, or "force-guiding," the fabric, which causes bias-cut fabrics to stretch or distort. You can also eliminate this potential problem by using a walking foot on your sewing machine.

Hint #2: Don't worry if your edges don't match perfectly when you are sewing them together. The seams are hidden inside the quilt. And the quilting stitches or ties help camouflage minor flaws. It's the total finished look that will make you proud to give or display your handiwork.

Hint #3: As you work, press all seam allowances toward the darker of the fabrics. This prevents seam allowances from being noticeable through lighter-colored fabrics.

1. After you have cut out all pieces, lay out one "Tumbling Block," consisting of three pieces (Fig. 6-5).

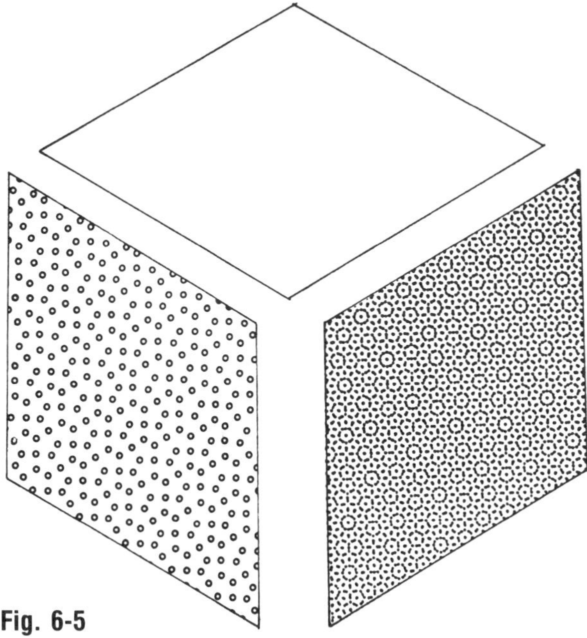

Fig. 6-5

2. Lay two of the three pieces right sides together and sew one seam, using a $\frac{3}{8}''$ seam allowance. *The trick with this pattern is to start your seam about $\frac{3}{8}''$ from the first angle and end the seam about $\frac{3}{8}''$ before the edge of the fabric (Fig. 6-6).*

Fig. 6-6

3. Open the first two pieces, then lay the third piece of fabric, right sides together, on one of the other two. Lay them flat, with the extra one out of the way. Starting with the end away from what will be the center of the block, sew toward the center of the block, using a $\frac{3}{8}''$ seam allowance and leaving a $\frac{3}{8}''$ space at the beginning and end of the seam (Fig. 6-7). Remember to back-tack the beginning and end of all seams.

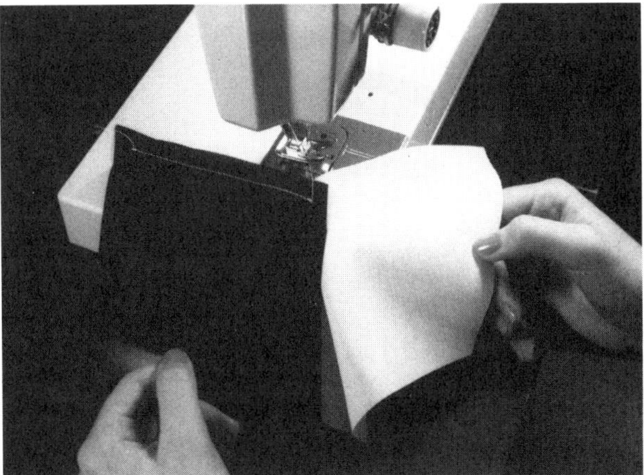

Fig. 6-7

4. Remove the block from your machine, and fold the entire piece in half, right sides together, so the remaining seam line is straight and even. (The first two seam lines will line up on top of each other.) Flatten the two pieces to be sewn, so that all seam allowances are pulled back and away from you. Starting at the end of where the first two seam lines meet, sew the remaining seam, again stopping about $\frac{3}{8}''$ from the end (Fig. 6-8).

Fig. 6-8

5. Press all seam allowances toward the darker fabric, and you will have a block that lies perfectly flat (Fig. 6-9).

Fig. 6-9

6. Continue to do this with the remaining pieces. When you have completed all blocks, line them up in horizontal rows. You will need the following number of blocks and rows:

Twin—4 rows of 4 blocks
3 rows of 5 blocks
Full/Queen—4 rows of 5 blocks
3 rows of 6 blocks
King—4 rows of 6 blocks
3 rows of 7 blocks

7. Sew the blocks together into horizontal rows. (Figure 6-10 shows the king size.) Every other row will be larger or smaller than the previous one. Again, leave a ⅜″ space at the beginning and ending of each seam.

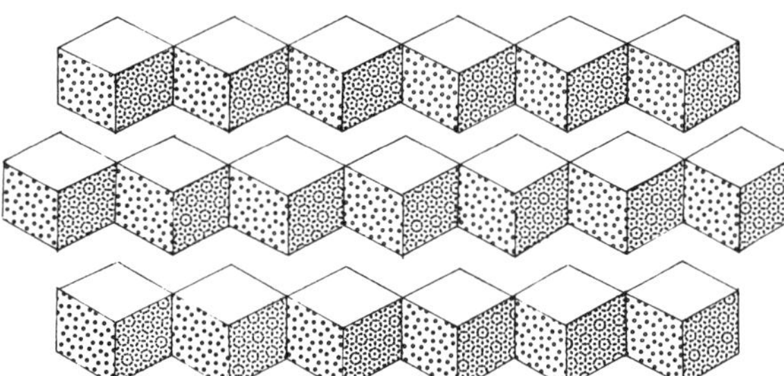

Fig. 6-10

8. Sew the rows together, as shown. Don't think of it as a long row of angles, but a series of little straight seams (Fig. 6-11). First lay the rows face up, so you can see where they will fit together. Then fold one on top of the other, right sides together, taking only the first seam, and seaming it as though it were only two pieces of fabric. When you reach the corner, back-tack the seam, lift your machine needle and presser foot, and reposition the next seam to be sewn, pulling seam allowances back and away from you. The unsewn edges of the seam allowances will allow you to "flex" the fabric, without pulling or stretching it. Continue doing this to the end of the row. All vertical seams should match when the rows are put together. You can stretch a bias-cut edge on one of the pieces to ease it into place, if necessary.

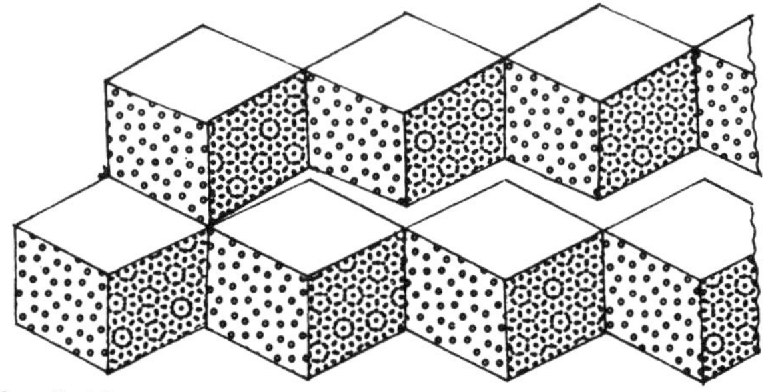

Fig. 6-11

9. You may have to go back and snip the corners of the seam allowance to allow the rows to lie flat, but, with practice, this won't even be necessary. Continue to sew the rows together until you have completed the face of your quilt (Fig. 6-12). Press all seams toward the darker fabric.

Fig. 6-12

10. The final step in completing your quilt face is to trim away all jagged edges (Fig. 6-13). After trimming the edges, your quilt face should measure approximately as follows:

Twin—92″ × 70″
Full/Queen—92″ × 88″
King—92″ × 104″

Fig. 6-13

Finishing the Quilt

1. Cut and seam the backing fabric, if necessary, to equal the size of your finished quilt top (see Figs. 6-1, 6-2).

2. Lay the backing (sheet, sheeting, or seamed fabric) right side down on a large, clean surface.

3. Place the polyester fiberfill or other batting on top of the backing.

4. Lay the quilt top right side up on the fiberfill. Hand baste, or pin using large safety pins, through all layers to hold them in place. (I prefer safety pins to straight pins because they save my hands and other body parts from pinpricks as I work.)

5. Using yarn, string, or ¹⁄₁₆″ ribbon, tie the layers firmly, or quilt the layers by hand or machine, as desired. Instructions follow.

6. Finish the edges, using bias tape or other decorative trim, as desired (Fig. 6-14). The edges can also be turned easily to the inside and sewn in place by machine (Fig. 6-15). You can insert piping, lace, or a ruffle at the edge with this method.

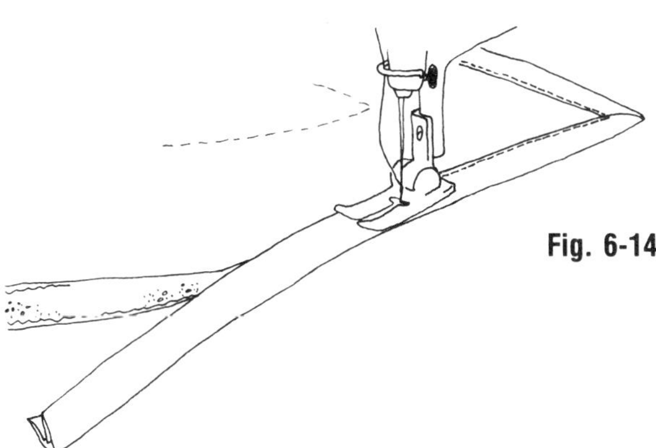

Fig. 6-14

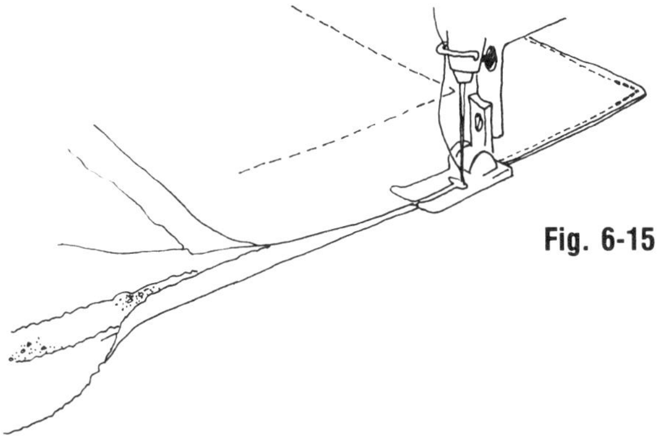

Fig. 6-15

To Add Bias Tape

There are many ways to apply a bias taped edge, but in general, it is easiest if you sew a seam around your entire project, using a narrow seam allowance, to keep the layers from stretching or shifting *before* you apply the bias tape.

Starting in the middle of one side of your project, and using long straight pins, pin the bias tape around the entire piece, overlapping and folding under the last edge where it meets with your starting point. When you get to a corner, tuck the excess flatly and neatly inside of itself, by gently pushing it to one side with pointed scissors or a pin. It may help to open the bias tape so it is flat when you get to a corner, then pinch the excess to guide it into the fold at the corner (Fig. 6-16). Hand baste or topstitch by machine over the miter.

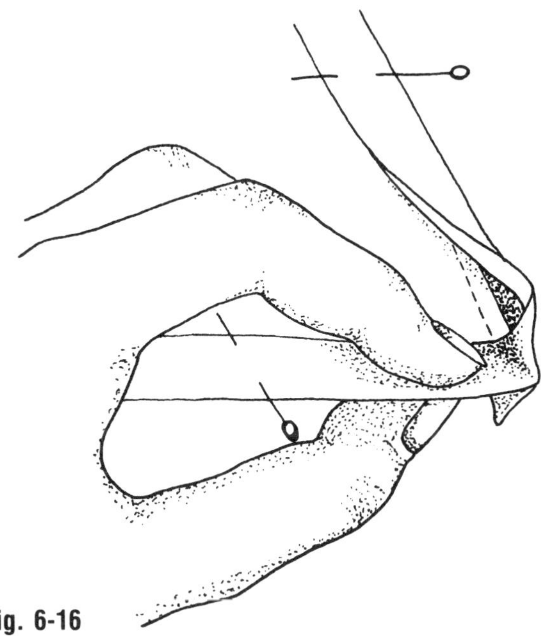

Fig. 6-16

To Tie Your Quilt

Tying your quilt is the easiest way to hold the layers together and provides a quick finish to your quilt. Baste or pin the layers of your quilt to hold them in place before starting to tie. It is not necessary to mark the points at which you will tie your quilt. Figure 6-17 shows where the ties should be placed.

Fig. 6-17

Thread a large needle (one with a large eye, such as a tapestry needle) with yarn, 1⁄16″ ribbon, or string (button or quilting thread also works well). Working from the top of the quilt, push the needle through all layers, drawing the thread through, but not all the way. Leave a 6″–8″ tail sticking out on top. About 1⁄8″–1⁄4″ from the first stitch, draw the needle back up (from the back to the front) through all layers. Cut the thread, again leaving a tail about 6″–8″ long. Tie these two tails tightly together, using a double or triple knot to hold the tie securely in place. You can make a bow with the excess, or simply trim the tails to about 1″.

To Quilt by Machine

After the layers are securely pinned or basted, roll up one-half of the quilt tightly enough to allow it to fit under the head of your sewing machine. You can safety-pin it closed or use bicycle clips to hold the roll. With larger quilts, you may need a friend to help guide the bulk through while you are quilting the center block.

Starting with the seams shown in Fig. 6-18, stitch "anchoring" quilt lines to hold all layers in place. This stitching will secure all layers of fabric and help keep the remainder of the quilt from shifting. It also helps to smooth the top and bottom toward you occasionally, with one hand above and one hand below, palms pressed gently together, and fingers spread.

Fig. 6-18

After you have stitched the lines shown in Fig. 6-18, continue quilting by machine, following the outline of the pattern by sewing along the seam lines of the pieced quilt top. Be sure to back-tack the beginning and end of each quilting seam. It is easiest to quilt all horizontal rows first, in the same thread color, then change to a thread color that matches one of the diagonal rows to finish your quilt. When quilting along a seam that joins a solid color to a print fabric, try to keep your quilting stitches on the printed fabric, to the side of the seam.

Today's polyester fiberfills don't clump or shift as much as natural battings, like wool or cotton, because of the resins that hold the polyester fibers together. The stitching lines suggested here are adequate to hold polyester fiberfill in place, but you may wish to add some extra quilting lines or ties if you are using pure wool or cotton batting.

Alternate Method of Finishing

1. Another method of finishing your quilt is to sew the face to the backing, right sides together, leaving the top edge open. Because these seams are so long, it helps to pin the edges together before sewing, to hold them in place. Be sure the back is cut to the exact size of the face before sewing them together.

2. Before turning right side out, lay your top and backing, which have been sewn together on three sides, right side down on a large, clean, flat surface. If you don't have a large enough floor space, lay it on as large a table as you can, with the open, unseamed end hanging over the edge of the table, and the bottom half of the quilt lying flat on the table. Place the polyester fiberfill on top and trim it to the exact size of the quilt.

3. Starting at the end opposite the opening, roll the entire quilt, like a sleeping bag, or jelly roll, until you have a long "tube" of fabric and batting.

4. Carefully reach inside the layers of fabric (between the face and backing), and slowly pull the tube inside-out, through the opening.

5. Slowly unwrap the quilt, which will open, filled with fiberfill, and with three of the edges finished. (Practice with a sock. First, roll the sock, starting at the toe, and pull the cuff back over the roll. Slowly unroll it from the inside out, reaching inside the sock, between the layers, and pulling gently on the roll.)

6. Lay the quilt on a large, flat surface, and pin or baste through all layers. Hand or machine quilt, or tie it, as described above.

7. Turn the remaining edges to the inside, pin to hold, and machine stitch to close.

Make a Crib Quilt or Wall Hanging (50″ × 40″)

Materials Needed

Face: 1¼ yards each of three fabrics

Backing: 1¾ yards of 44/45″ wide fabric

Polyester fiberfill to 54″ × 44″

Thread (for piecing your quilt face, as well as for hand or machine quilting, if desired)

String, yarn, or ¹⁄₁₆″ ribbon for tying your quilt, if you prefer

Graph paper or plain paper (which you have scored with 1″ squares) for pattern making

1. See "Getting Started" in the instructions for the large quilts. For this size quilt you can trace your pattern piece directly from the template on page 6-16. **Do not add seam allowances.** Cut out the pattern, then cut 44 pieces of each of three fabrics. Be sure to use your rotary cutting tools to cut several layers of fabric at the same time.

2. Follow Steps 1 through 5 in the piecing instructions for completing the "Tumbling Blocks," page 6-4. Continue until you have pieced 44 blocks.

3. Sew the blocks into four horizontal rows of five blocks and four rows of six blocks (see Steps 7, 8, and 9, page 6-6). Starting with a row of six blocks, and alternating the rows, sew them together as described for the large quilts.

4. Trim the finished piece to a rectangle approximately 50″ × 40″.

5. Refer to "Finishing the Quilt" in the instructions for the large quilts to complete the crib quilt or wall hanging. (This pattern is simply a miniature version of the large quilt.)

You will probably want to make loops of fabric to sew to the top of your finished wall hanging project or just behind the upper edge (hidden) to allow for a dowel rod to hang it.

To Make the Loops

For **hidden loops**, cut three pieces of fabric 1½″ × 4″. Fold the long edges inward to meet at the center, then fold the whole strip in half lengthwise. Using a straight stitch, sew through all layers along the "open" edge to make a small "ribbon" of fabric. Attach one in the middle of the upper edge of the wall hanging, and the remaining two at either side on the upper edge. Tack these to the wall hanging through all layers using your sewing machine, or hand sew them in place.

For **decorative loops**, cut three pieces of matching fabric 3″ × 5″. Fold these in half, right sides together, to create 1½″ × 5″ pieces. Using a ⅜″ seam allowance, sew a straight line down the 5″ raw edge. Turn these tubes right side out and press so the seam is centered on one side. Fold these in half widthwise to hide the seam. Attach to the top of your wall hanging by machine, spacing the loops evenly (Fig. 6-19).

Fig. 6-19

For **bow loops**, cut three pieces of wide ribbon, each 24″ long. Fold these in half and tack them to the top edge of your wall hanging by hand or machine, evenly spaced. Tie these loosely around a decorative pole or dowel rod.

This project finishes to a perfect size for use as a table topper, lap quilt, or sofa throw.

Make a 16″ Throw Pillow

Fabric Requirements

Face: Use leftover scrap from quilt or ¼ yard each of three fabrics

Back: ½ yard of a matching fabric

Ruffle or cord (if desired): ⅝ yard

1. Trace the pillow pattern piece from page 6-16 onto tracing paper. **Do not add seam allowances.** Cut out the pattern, then cut 14 pieces of each of three fabrics.

2. Follow Steps 1 through 5 in the piecing instructions for completing the "Tumbling Blocks," page 6-4. Continue until 14 blocks are pieced.

3. Sew the blocks into two rows of four blocks and two rows of three. Alternate the rows and sew them together. (See Steps 7, 8, and 9, page 6-6).

4. Cut this finished piece into a square approximately 17″ square.

5. You may wish to first quilt the pillow face by layering it with a plain muslin backing and fiberfill, cut to the same size as the face, then hand or machine quilt along the seams. This is not necessary, simply a matter of preference.

6. See the instructions for making and applying ruffling and bias cording, page 6-13. With raw edges together, and with a ⅜″ seam allowance, sew bias cording (Fig. 6-20) or a ruffle (Fig. 6-21) around the entire pillow face. You will need about 2 yards of bias cording or finished ruffling to go around the pillow. For a knife-edge pillow, with no extra trim, you can eliminate this step.

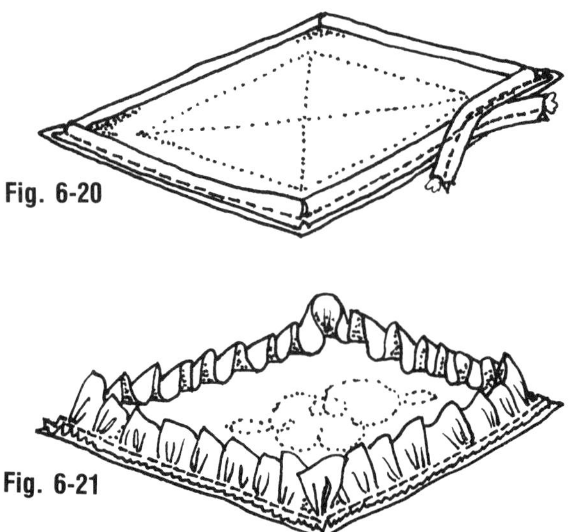

Fig. 6-20

Fig. 6-21

7. Cut two pieces of a backing fabric, 10″ × 17″. Finish one 17″ edge on each of these two pieces with a double-folded hem, machine stitched.

8. Lay the pillow right side up, with ruffle or cording toward the center. Place the backing right side down, on the pillow, overlapping the finished edges evenly in the center. Pin around the edges (Fig. 6-22).

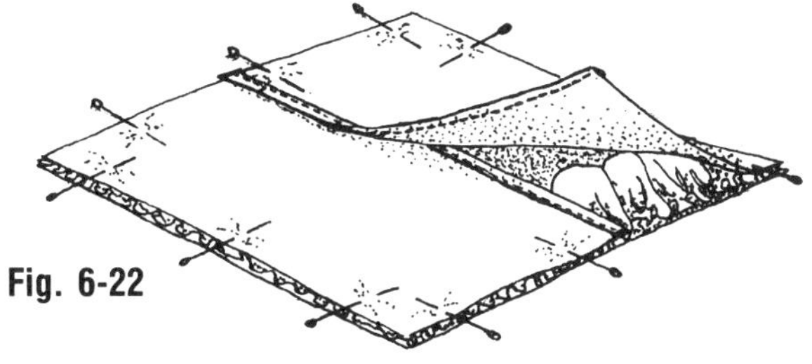

Fig. 6-22

9. Sew around the entire pillow, following the seam used to sew the cording or ruffle in place, or using a ⅜″ seam allowance. Turn inside out through the overlapped backing. Trim away any excess around the seams before turning.

10. Insert a 15″ or 16″ pillow form.

Make Your Own 15″–16″ Pillow Form

1. Save your scrap fiberfill.

2. Cut two 18″ squares of any white or ivory fabric.

3. Sew these together on three sides, using a ½″ seam allowance. Turn right side out.

4. Cut two 17″ squares of leftover fiberfill, and carefully slide them into the pillow cover. Continue to stuff smaller bits of fiberfill between the squares, until the pillow is plump, but not too hard.

5. To finish, whipstitch the opening by hand. I call this a 15″–16″ finished size because the finished size will vary according to the plumpness of the pillow.

Make a Removable Chair Pad Cover

Note: An additional ⅓ yard of one of the fabrics is required for each chair pad.

1. Complete the 16″ pillow cover as explained above in "Make a 16″ Throw Pillow."

2. Cut two strips of fabric, 44″ × 5″. With a roll-hem attachment for your sewing machine, or a narrow double fold, hem around all sides of both strips. You may wish to fold one corner of each end to the inside and machine stitch to hold in place, to create pointed ends. Fold each strip in half, matching the two short ends, to create two tie ends, and pinch or pleat at the fold to gather. At what will be the back two corners, machine stitch the ties to the pillow cover, on the underside of the finished pillow, under the ruffle (Fig. 6-23).

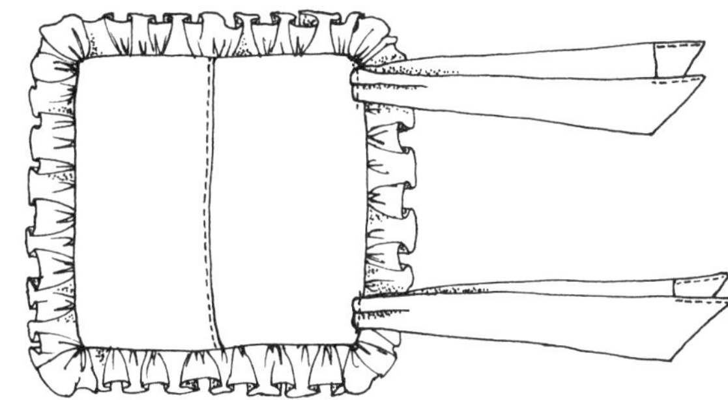

Fig. 6-23

3. To make a removable chair pad insert, purchase or make a 15″–16″ pillow form. With a long needle and double heavy-duty thread, run the thread through the center of the pillow form, leaving a "tail" of thread about 6″ long. Bring the needle back through about ½″ from the first stitch, and tie the ends of the thread, pulling tightly to form a "tuft" in the center.

Two matching chair pads with inserts make a lovely rocker set.

Make a Standard Pillow Sham

Fabric Requirements

Face: Use leftover scrap from quilt or ½ yard each of three fabrics

Back: ⅔ yard

Ruffle (if desired): ⅞ yard

1. See "Getting Started" in the instructions for the large quilts. Trace the pillow sham pattern piece from page 6-16 onto tracing paper. **Do not add seam allowances**. Cut out the pattern, then cut 13 pieces of each of two fabrics, and 18 pieces of the third fabric.

2. Follow Steps 1 through 5 in the piecing instructions for completing the "Tumbling Blocks," page 6-4. Continue until you have pieced 13 blocks.

3. Sew the blocks into two rows of four blocks and one row of five. Place the row of five blocks between the rows of four and sew these rows together as described in Steps 7, 8, and 9, page 6-6. Add the remaining five pieces as shown (Fig. 6-24).

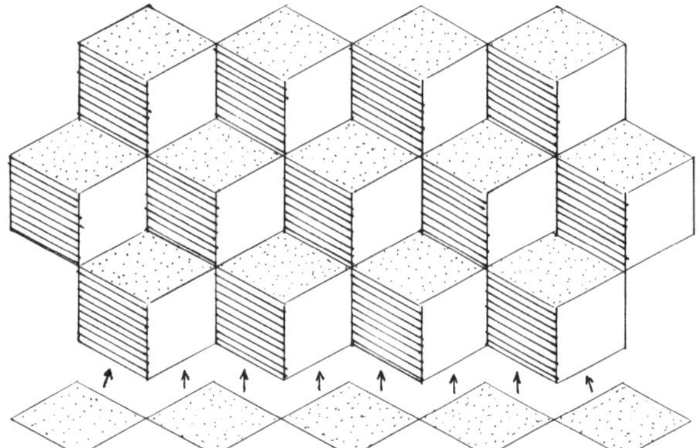

Fig. 6-24

4. Cut this finished piece into a rectangle approximately 22″ × 28″.

5. You may wish to first quilt the sham face by layering it with a plain muslin backing and fiberfill, cut to the same size as the face, then hand or machine quilt along the seams. This is not necessary, simply a matter of preference.

6. See the instructions for making and applying ruffling and bias cording on page 6-13. With raw edges together, sew bias cording or a ruffle around the entire sham face (see Figs. 6-20, 6-21). You will need about 3 yards of bias cording or finished ruffling to go around the pillow sham. This is sewn to the right side of the pillow sham. For a knife-edge pillow sham, with no extra trim, you can eliminate this step.

7. Cut two pieces of a backing fabric, 16″ × 24″, finishing one 24″ edge on each piece with a narrow double-folded hem, machine stitched.

8. Lay the pillow sham right side up, with ruffle or cording pressed toward the center. Place the backing right side down, on the sham, overlapping the finished edges evenly in the center. Pin around the edges (see Fig. 6-22).

9. Sew around the entire pillow sham, following the seam used to sew the ruffling and/or cording in place Turn inside out through the overlapped backing. Trim away any excess around the seams before turning right side out (Fig. 6-25).

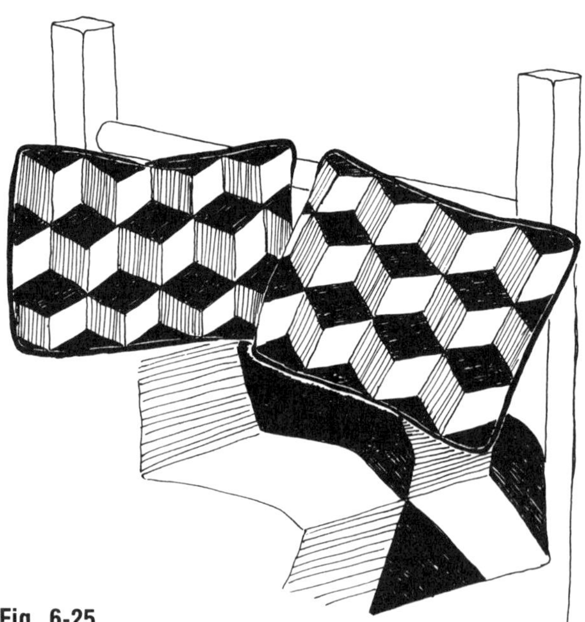

Fig. 6-25

How to Make Matching Ruffling and Bias Cording for Pillows, Shams, and Chair Pads

Ruffling

You will need about 5/8 yard of extra fabric for ruffles around pillows and chair pads. You will need about 7/8 yard for pillow shams.

1. From the width of the fabric (44/45″) cut three 7″ strips (four strips for pillow shams), and sew them together on the short ends to make a long circle of fabric. Press the seam allowances open (Fig. 6-26).

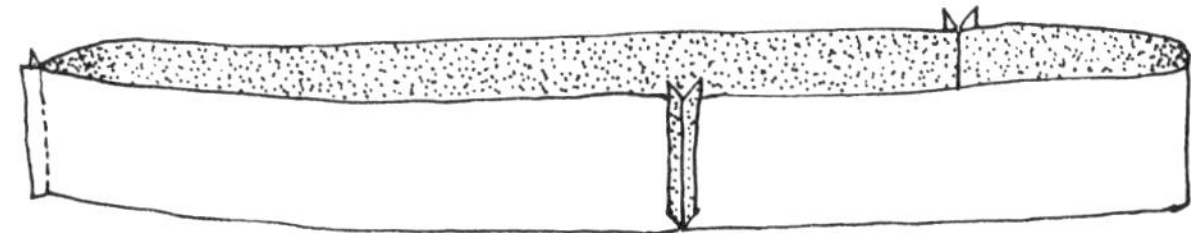

Fig. 6-26

2. Fold the circle in half lengthwise, so the raw edges meet, and right sides face out. Press.

3. With a wide basting stitch, sew about 1/4″ from the raw edge (Fig. 6-27).

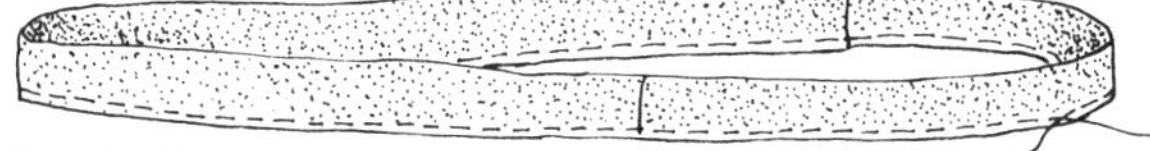

Fig. 6-27

4. Divide the circle equally into quarters, identifying the quarter marks with a straight pin. Pin the circle to the center of each straight edge on all four sides of your project, using the pins that mark the quarters to hold the ruffle in place.

5. Pull the basting stitch until the circle gathers evenly into a ruffle equal to the size of the project you are working on. Use straight pins to hold the ruffle in place around the outer edge of the project, raw edges together, as you gather it to fit.

Bias Cording

You will need 5/8 yard of matching fabric to make your own bias cording.

1. Cut a 1½″-wide strip of fabric on the bias. The strip of bias-cut fabric should be several inches longer than the measurement around the edge of the project you wish to trim.

2. Using purchased cording, wrap the bias strip around the cording so that wrong sides and raw edges meet. With a zipper foot attachment, stitch close to the cord, but not too snug, through both layers of fabric (Fig. 6-28).

3. The simplest application of the finished bias cording is to begin sewing it on one straight edge, keeping the raw edges of the bias tape and your project even, but with the starting end angled off the edge. Sew around the entire project, clipping the seam allowance of the bias tape at the corners. When you reach your starting point, overlap the bias tape, sewing over the angled end, and carefully angle the final end to sew it off the edge (see Fig. 6-20). Clip it to trim.

You may also apply bias tape by starting in the middle of one side, but start your seam about 2″ from the end of the bias tape. Sew all around as described above, but when you get to where you started, open the seam on the 2″ tail of the bias tape and pull back the fabric to show the cord. Clip off the 2″ of cord, and fold the fabric that is left in half, to create a 1″ tail (fold the fabric to the inside, so that only the right side shows). Cut the other end of the bias tape so it ends exactly where the first cord now starts. Wrap the folded bias tape fabric around this raw edge, and finish your seam.

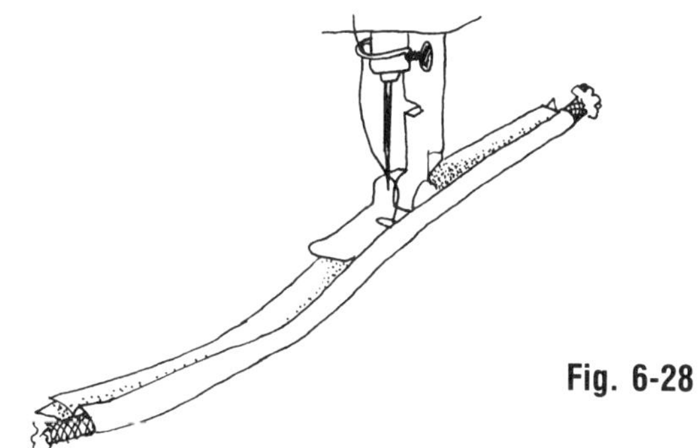

Fig. 6-28

Make a Placemat

Fabric Requirements

Face: Use leftover scrap from quilt or ¼ yard each of three fabrics

Back: ½ yard of fabric will allow enough for *two* placemats

1. Trace the pillow pattern piece from page 6-16 onto tracing paper. Cut out the pattern, then cut 16 of each of your three fabrics.

2. Follow Steps 1 through 5 in the piecing instructions for completing the "Tumbling Blocks," page 6-4. Continue until 16 blocks are pieced.

3. Sew the blocks into four rows of four blocks. Sew these rows together as described in Steps 7, 8, and 9, page 6-6.

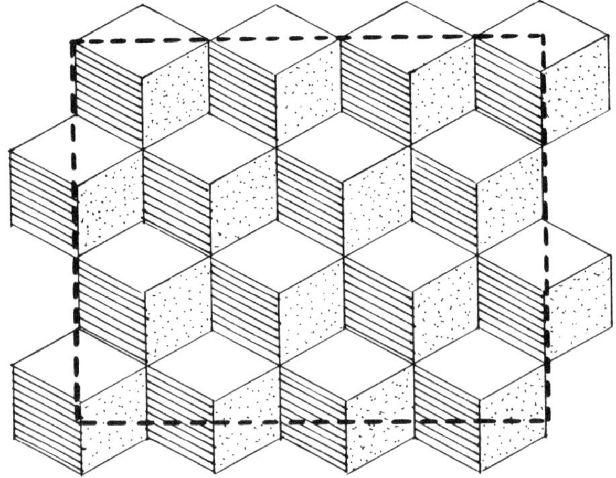

Fig. 6-29

4. Cut this finished piece into a rectangle approximately 17″ × 20″ (Fig. 6-29).

5. Cut a rectangle of backing fabric 17″ × 20″. Place the back and the pieced face right sides together. Sew together with a ⅜″ seam allowance all around, except for a 4″ opening centered on one of the seams. Clip the corners and turn inside out through the opening. Hand or machine stitch the opening and press all around.

6. To minimize raveling or fraying of the seams on the inside when these are washed, you may wish to "quilt" along the seam lines, even though these do not have fiberfill. (You may add fiberfill, if you wish.)

Optika Pattern Guide for Twin, Full/Queen, and King Quilts

Dimensions include ⅜″ seam allowance.

Cut the following number of pieces of each of your three fabrics:

For twin size, cut 31 pieces of each color.
For full/queen size, cut 38 pieces of each color.
For king size, cut 45 pieces of each color.

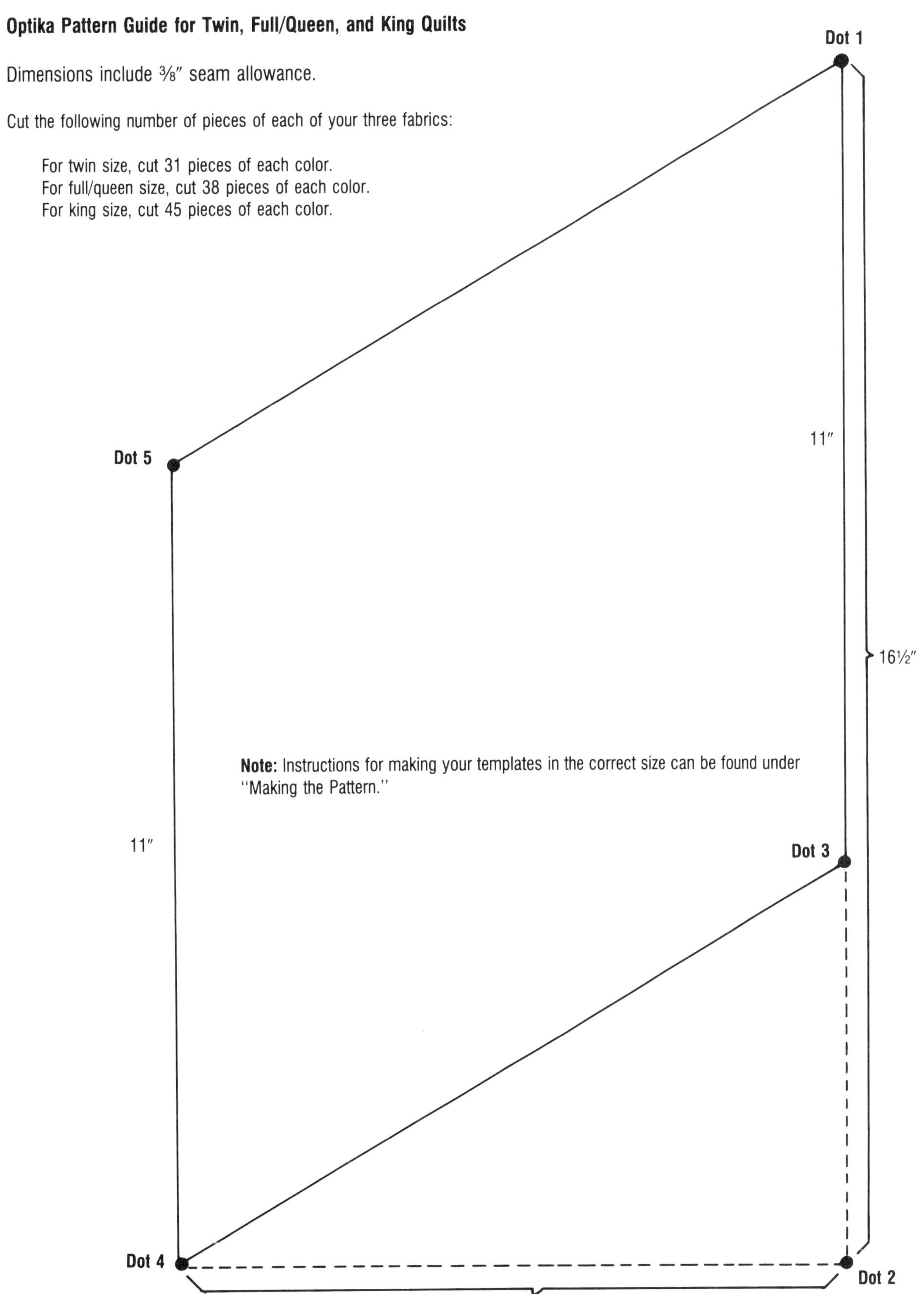

Optika Templates

For the crib quilt/wall hanging, and the pillow sham, use the larger template given here. For the crib quilt and wall hanging, cut 44 pieces of each of three fabrics. For the pillow sham, cut 13 pieces of each of two fabrics and 18 pieces of the third fabric.

For the 16″ pillow, the chair pad, and the placemat, use the smaller template given here. For the pillow and chair pad, cut 14 pieces each of three fabrics. For the placemat, cut 16 pieces each of three fabrics.

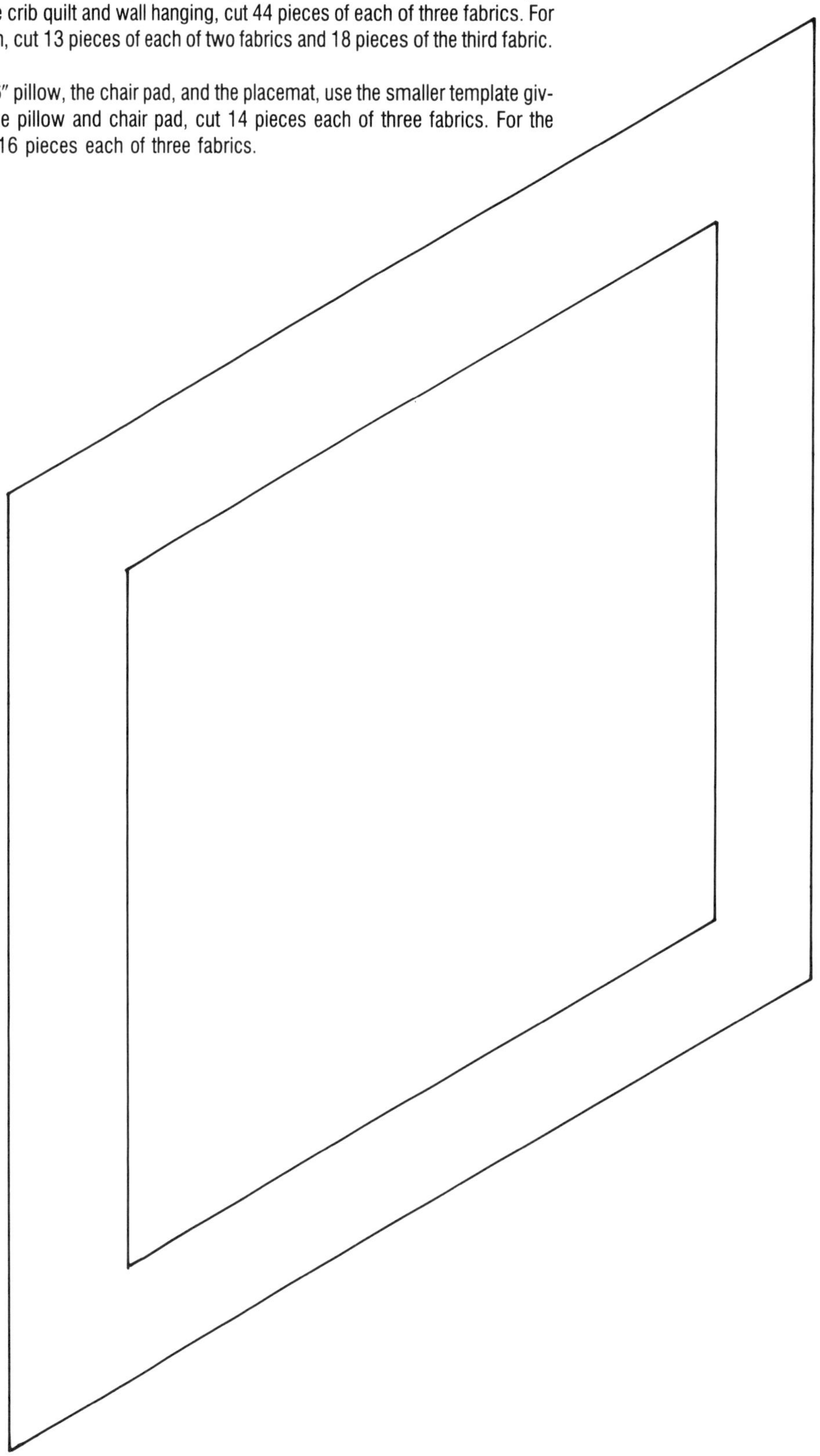